Sefer

Mivchar HaPeninim

A Choice of Pearls

ספר מבחר הפנינים

Philosopher Rabbi

Solomon ibn Gabirol

There is no known book without mistakes. Therefore, I ask in every language of application if anyone has any questions, comments, clarifications, corrections, please send to: **simchatchaim@yahoo.com**

All material used in this section may not be used for commercial purposes, but only for study and teaching.

To get this book or books and information Email me at:

simchatchaim@yahoo.com

Copyright©All Rights Reserved to

www.simchatchaim.com

YB"S©All rights reserved to the Editor

First Edition 2023

Mivchar   HaPeninim

Rabbi Solomon Ibn Gabirel

This great Hebrew poet and philosopher was born in Malaga, Spain, about the year 4782, [1021], and died in Valencia, Spain, at the age of 36 or 37.

Despite his very short life, Rabbi Solomon ibn Gabirel won great fame during his own lifetime, and even more so after his death when his writings became more widely known.

His father Yehuda, was a native of the famous city of Cordova which was at the time under Arab domination. About ten years before Solomon's birth, when war broke out in that part of the Spanish peninsula, his father moved to Saragossa, also under Arab domination. Later they moved to Malaga, where Rabbi Solomon was born.

Losing his parents at an early age, Rabbi Solomon nevertheless continued his studies of the Talmud, in which he found his only solace. The young Rabbi Solomon was an ardent scholar and became very proficient in the Hebrew as well as Arabic languages and grammar. He also studied astronomy, geometry, and philosophy.

Rabbi Solomon Ibn Gabirel began writing Hebrew poetry when he was very young. At the age of 16 he wrote a famous poem beginning with the words, "I am the master, and Song is my slave." This poem entitled **Azharoth**, is based on the Taryag [613] commandments of the Torah, and was included in the Shavuoth service of many congregations.

In that year, the famous Rav Hal Gaon died in Babylon, and Solomon ibn Gabirel wrote four dirges [obituary poems] on the passing of this great scholar.

Rabbi Solomon Ibn Gabirel sang the praises of Rabbi Samuel Hanagid and also of another Jewish minister, Jekuthiel ibn Hasan of Saragossa. The latter became Rabbi Solomon ibn Gabirel's friend and patron. Unfortunately, Rabbi Ibn Hasan met with a violent death through a false accusation by his enemies. Rabbi Solomon Ibn Gabirel, who was about eighteen or nineteen years old at that time, composed a touching eulogy on the loss of his friend.

A number of Rabbi Solomon ibn Gabirel's religious hymns were included in the prayer book. These include in addition to **Azharoth** mentioned above, his Shir Hakovod [Song of Glory], and - Shir Hayichud [Song of Unity]. Another of his famous poems is Kether Malchuth [Royal Crown]. Rabbi Solomon Ibn Gabirel also wrote "Kinoth" [dirges] on the destruction of the Temple and the plight of Israel. His most famous book he wrote was The Improvement of the Moral Qualities. This book discusses Jewish philosophy of the soul and its relations to the four elements of the world.

Rabbi Solomon Ibn Gabirel's life was not a very happy one, for he was a lonesome young man with a sensitive soul. He did not hesitate to use his poetic gifts in denouncing the lack of Jewish feeling on the part of some prominent members of his community. As a result of this, he acquired many enemies who made life in Saragossa miserable for him. Eventually, Rabbi Solomon Ibn Gabirel was banished from his native town and spent some years as a luckless wanderer, suffering many hardships. No wonder there is a touch of bitterness in his poems, but this is often coupled with a sense of humor.

At the age of only 23, Rabbi Solomon Ibn Gabirel wrote his book - Tikkun Middoth Hanefesh, [Improvement of the Qualities of the Soul].

About the same time, he also wrote - **Mivchar Hapeninim**, [Choice of Pearls].

Both Books were written in Arabic and subsequently translated into Hebrew by Rabbi Yehuda ibn Tibbon. In these books, Rabbi Solomon Ibn Gabirel presents a collection of moral sayings and maxims from Jewish as well as non-Jewish sources.

The manner of Rabbi Solomon ibn Gabirel's death is shrouded in mystery. Legend has it that he was trampled to death by an Arab horseman, much in the same way that Rabbi Yehuda Halevi lost his life.

Mivchar   HaPeninim

Rabbi Solomon Ibn Gabirol
statue in Málaga, Spain

Mivchar HaPeninim
A choice of pearls

Rabbi
Solomon ibn Gabirol

Chapter 1

1. The sage says, Wisdom is the means by which the wise thoroughly evince their gratitude towards their Creator, by which they become his true worshippers during life, and obtain a good name after death.

2. Nothing, says he, tends so greatly to render the intellect acute as instruction and wisdom, nor is anything more calculated to manifest true knowledge, than good conduct.

3. The questions of the wise are indicative of wisdom, affability towards mankind denotes intellect, and economy is equivalent to half a subsistence.

4. Who is the most fitted to rule, The wise man who has succeeded to power or dominion, or the king searching after wisdom.

5. The wise and the just should fear no man, for the pious fear none but God.

Mivchar HaPeninim

6. The means of attaining wisdom once neglected, are irrecoverable, but wisdom leans to those who seek her.

7. He who strives after wisdom and morality, strives for a diadem of golden words and sublime expressions, woven by the poet to deck the brow of his dearest and most deserving friends.

8. The pursuit of wisdom arrests the commission of iniquities, and inclines man to despise this transient world, and to love the everlasting one.

9. The sage was wont to say, Wisdom is incompatible with the banquet and the revel - her presence is not welcomed there.

10. He whom the Creator has endowed with wisdom will never be dismayed in trouble or distress, for the end of wisdom is peace and tranquility, whilst that of gold and silver is grief and vexation.

11. I do not vainly hope, said the sage, to attain wisdom in its fullest extent, but solely to escape the imputation of ignorance, a principle imperative on every rational being.

12. He also counsels his son not to be wise in words, but in deeds, for practical wisdom

Mivchar HaPeninim

benefits man hereafter, whilst wordy wisdom extends not beyond this transient world.

13. He likewise enjoined his son to court the society of the wise, For, said he, they will award praise to thy knowledge, instruct thine inexperience, and their commendations will benefit thee.

14. He used to say, it is peculiar to the ignorant to be fettered by death, - wisdom must loosen the shackles.

15. Wisdom, excites us to activity, and activity induces wisdom, yet it is less unpardonable to neglect wisdom from ignorance, than to neglect it from disdain.

16. To the question, how he became wiser than his companions, he replied, Because, I spent more in oil than they in wine.

17. Man without wisdom, is like a house without a foundation.

18. He who is renowned for wisdom is regarded with respect.

19. Be silent, and thou are safe, be attentive, and thou wilt be instructed.

20. Nothing is more useful to man, than to

be conscious of his station, the extent of his wisdom, and power of perception, by these only must his words be regulated.

21. During the pursuit of wisdom man may be termed wise, but the conceit of having attained it, renders him a fool.

22. The most precious bequest is wisdom, for wealth is obtained by wisdom, but is forfeited by folly, to the inevitable sacrifice of all.

23. He who humbles himself in quest of wisdom, will in turn be honored by those who seek it of him.

24. Wisdom constitutes the noblest pedigree, and love the closest - tie.

25. Kings judge the world, but the wise judge kings.

26. Wisdom is the delight of the wise - folly of the fool.

27. Admirable is the deed crowned by wisdom, delightful is wisdom crowned by practice, yet more excellent still is practice decked by gentleness and grace.

Mivchar   HaPeninim

28. There is no happier union than that of modesty with wisdom, and power with clemency.

29. Robustness and obesity are seldom the portion of the devotee to study and religion.

30. The wise man thus enjoined his son - Endeavour to be wise, to learn, and to be attentive, neglect these and thou art undone.

31. Scruple not to be enlightened on subjects of which thou art ignorant, so that thou be spared the blush of confessing thine own folly.

32. Know that the connexion of reason and faith is as that of the head and the body, for as the loss of the head necessarily entails that of the body, so does the loss of reason involve that of faith.

33. Man's worth is estimated according to his knowledge.

34. Let not the honour bestowed on thy wealth and power elate thee, for that honour vanishes when they disappear, but gratifying indeed is that honour elicited by wisdom, fear of the Lord, and morality.

35. The wise of the earth resemble the luminaries of the heavens.

Mivchar HaPeninim

36. It was asked of the sage - Who are superior, the wise or the rich, the wise, was his reply.

37. But why, objected the querist, are the wise more frequently at the door of the rich, than the rich at the door of the wise, Because, rejoined he, the wise know the value of wealth, whilst the opulent do not know that of wisdom.

38. The true believer only condescends to flatter when he pursues wisdom.

39. The first step to wisdom is silence, the second attention, the third memory, the fourth activity, the fifth study.

40. In the assembly of the wise be more disposed to listen than to speak.

41. God will bestow wisdom on those who truly revere him, and her outpourings will be conveyed from the heart to the tongue.

42. He alone can be considered wise who possesses the following three qualities, not to despise inferiors in their endeavours to attain wisdom, not to envy those who are wealthier than himself, and not to barter his wisdom for lucre.

43. Seek wisdom even in the language of

Mivchar HaPeninim

folly, but impart it unsparingly and with discretion, after the manner of the liberal.

44. Man's most estimable peculiarity is an inquiring mind.

45. He who seeks wisdom in the garb of bashfulness, will be enveloped in the attire of folly, let therefore the votary of wisdom divest himself of that garb.

46. Arrogance diminishes wisdom.

47. The wise man continues - Wisdom is ever found accompanied by diffidence and patience, and the interrogatories of the fool by meanness and pride.

48. Timidity is incompatible with hope, as is bash fulness with wisdom.

49. It is imperative on the true believer to repair the loss of wisdom, even through the medium of the sceptic.

50. The sage recommended his son, to be untiring in the acquisition of wisdom, for though, said he, thou mayest be subordinate to some, thou will prove superior to others.

51. How degrading is folly in old age.

Mivchar HaPeninim

52. Impart learning to the ignorant, and receive it from the erudite, thus, wilt thou acquire that of which thou art ignorant, and retain that which thou hast acquired.

53. Wisdom sought after in old age fades like letters traced in sand, whilst that obtained in youth may endure like characters engraved in stone.

54. Withhold knowledge from the unworthy, lest you wrong wisdom, refuse it not from the deserving, lest you wrong them, nor requite the wicked according to their wickedness, lest you forfeit the reward of your Creator.

55. Obedience consists in our promptitude to observe the commands enjoined on us, and in abstaining from things prohibited to us.

56. Poverty can never disgrace the wise man, nor will lust subdue him.

57. The sage who was once contradicted by an illiterate man, thus replied - Hades thou been able to appreciate my words, thou wouldst have acquiesced in them, or had I not penetrated thy meaning, I should have condemned thee, but though thy ignorance merit reproach, I who know thy folly acquit thee.

Mivchar HaPeninim

58. Wisdom lying dormant is like an unproductive treasure.

59. Wisdom may be comprised under the following two heads - the wisdom of the heart which is of real effect, and the wisdom of the tongue unaccompanied by deeds, the one is the most useful, the other causes man to incur the reproach of his maker.

60. Mankind may be classified thus.
1st. the learned man, who is conscious of his learning, he may be termed truly wise - of him shalt thou seek knowledge.
2nd. If learned, but unconscious of his learning, remind him of it [that he may not further forget it].
3rd. If ignorant, and aware of his ignorance, instruct him.
4th. But if ignorant, and assuming to be learned, he is a fool, dismiss him.

61. He used to say, pretend not to that of which thou art ignorant, lest thine actual knowledge should be discredited.

62. No virtues lead to more felicitous results than faith in God, honour to parents, love to wisdom, and attention to moral instruction.

63. The fool is prone to impute his faults to others, the votary of moral improvement will freely confess his errors, but the truly pious and wise will endeavour to avoid either.

64. Be ready to accept truth from whomsoever it may emanate, even from inferiors.

65. He who would philosophize without wisdom, may be compared to an ass, which moves round the millstone, without advancing beyond it.

66. The sage observed, Pity the noble hearted who has fallen, the rich that has become reduced, and the wise, whose lot is cast amongst the fools.

67. None deserves our pity more than the wise who has become subjected to the judgment of fools.

68. Cast not pearls to the swine, for they are valueless to them, intrust not wisdom to him, who cannot appreciate it, for wisdom is dearer than pearls, and he who seeks it not, is inferior to the brute.

69. The sage observes - The exhortation of the wise, unaccompanied by practice, falls on the heart as rain on stone, and he whose words are at variance with his deeds disgraces himself, hence, words which emanate not from

Mivchar   HaPeninim

the heart can never penetrate the ear.

70. We can only be sensible of the errors of our preceptors, when we have heard their doctrines contested.

71. On being asked, whether the acquisition of knowledge befits old age, the sage replied, if ignorance be a disgrace, then must learning be an ornament.

72. True dignity will never scorn the performance of the following four duties.
>**1st**. To rise from his seat before his parent.
>**2nd**. To wait upon his guest.
>**3rd**. To devote personal attention to the state of his horses, equipage, and property, though he may have a hundred servants to do it.
>**4th**. To respect the learned, so as to profit by their wisdom.

73. The society of the wise confers honour, that of the ignorant contempt.

74. Avoid the ignorant who feign piety, and the learned man who is sinful.

75. Seek wisdom with the avidity with which thou wouldst search for hidden treasures, for it is more precious than gold and silver.

Mivchar HaPeninim

Chapter 2

76. The wise man was asked, who is the Creator, he replied, to discuss a subject which cannot be comprehended is folly, and to dispute on matters beyond the power of conception is sinful.

77. He used to say, A wise man chancing to enter an assembly of disputants, addressed them as follows - Your argument will never lead to a satisfactory result. On being asked, Wherefore, he replied, A successful result would imply unanimity of opinion.

Mivchar HaPeninim

Chapter 3

78. The wise man says, Diffidence is the diadem of the intelligent, the characteristic of the fool is boldness, and the result of all diffidence is peace.

79. He used to say, Evil words fall harmlessly on my ears. On being asked for a reason, he answered, it is from the dread of hearing epithets harsher still.

80. Silence is the reply adapted to folly.

81. He who is deficient of the following three qualities cannot be said to have the least idea of faith - First, meekness to reply to folly, second, piety to guard from sin, and third, gentleness to reconcile himself with mankind.

82. A certain man thus addressed a philosopher - Mankind, I perceive, are prone to injure, hence mine ardent desire to shun their intercourse. The sage, however, replied, do not so, for thou canst as little dispense with them as they with thee, but seem in their presence as one who hears and is deaf, who speaks and is dumb, and who sees and is blind.

83. There is no merit in sparing pain to others, but in our efforts to bear it patiently.

Mivchar HaPeninim

84. It was asked of the sage, in what one virtue are all the rest comprised, Patience, was his answer. And in what single vice are all others concentrated, Vindictiveness.

85. A wise man having been treated with contumely, one of his disciples asked permission to retaliate. No, replied the sage, he is no wise man who authorizes another to inflict injury.

86. He who possesses abundant patience and meekness will witness the diminution of his oppressors, and the increase of his supporters.

87. It was a favourite observation of the sage, that discord ends in regret, and meekness in harmony.

88. The unassuming acquire superiority, and the reflective wisdom.

89. I never prided myself on being a more rigorous scrutinizer to my least delinquencies, Vide Appendix. than to the heaviest transgressions of my fellow-creatures.

90. He who cannot control his anger does not possess perfect wisdom.

91. Silence is the fittest reply to folly.

92. On asking the sage who may be truly

termed a hero, he replied, He who can requite folly with meekness, and subdue his anger.

93. For how can he rule over others who cannot govern himself.

94. Humility is often made the butt of folly.

95. Impatience under one wrong will necessitate the endurance of many more.

96. Power and victory are often the lot of the humble.

97. Modesty enlists mankind to combat the assaults of folly.

98. A wise man thus reproached one who vituperated him - Be lenient to my faults, and leave room for reconciliation.

99. To bear quietly that which is unpleasant, will prevent harsher epithets.

100. I find diffidence more valuable than the aid of mankind.

101. A sage was annoyed by the abuse of one who followed him to his door, heaping on him a torrent of reproachful epithets. Be brief, said the philosopher, and leave me, lest thy slander should be overheard by my menials, who may

Mivchar HaPeninim

then compel thee to hear that which may displease thee, and repay thy slander with castigation.

102. The following observation was made by the sage who was abused by a querulous man - Thou hast omitted none of my failings of which thou art cognizant, but those which God knows of thee are still more.

103. Error is incompatible with regularity. Vide Appendix.

104. Patience under ordinary misfortunes lightens troubles more serious.

105. To choose good is to avoid evil.

Chapter 4

106. The sage observes, Pardon is alike due to the sordid and the generous.

107. Extend thy pardon to him who wronged thee, and thy charity to him who has withheld it from thee.

108. Sins confessed is a solicitation for forgiveness.

109. Confess thy sins and crave forgiveness, for denial doubles the offence.

110. Pardon the sin of thy friend, and contend not with thine enemy.

111. Revenge produces sorrow, pardon gladness.

112. It is recorded of a king, who had decreed the execution of a band of malefactors, that one of the condemned craved forgiveness in the following expressive terms. Wicked as we were, O lord king, in committing sins, yet let not that preclude the exercise of thy royal clemency to spare our wretched lives. These expressive words pleased the king, who tempered justice with mercy, and granted pardon.

Mivchar HaPeninim

113. A certain king ordered the execution of a philosopher, one of the counsellors pleaded for him in the following terms - My lord, though thy power may enable thee to accomplish an act, yet can it ever enable thee to undo one, the king reflected and revoked the fatal decree.

Mivchar HaPeninim

Chapter 5

114. The sage observed, reflection ensures safety, precipitancy regret.

115. Reflections may produce prosperity, haste, misfortune.

116. The fleet rider is not secure from stumbling.

117. We often accelerate by reflection, whilst we retard by impetuosity.

Mivchar HaPeninim

Chapter 6

118. They asked the wise man, why do we not perceive in thee the least trace of care, Because, replied he, the loss of fortune never occasioned me regret.

119. He used to observe, everything must be defined by a certain standard.

120. Being asked, for instance, how he would define confidence, by faith, was his reply, to the further interrogatory, as to what constitutes faith, he rejoined, to fear no man, to rely on God, to bear patiently his visitations, and to be submissive to his decrees.

121. Joy and ease are associated with equanimity, care and vexation with impetuosity.

122. Nothing transcends faith - it is our safeguard against the direct hardships of poverty, sickness, and dread, this protection faith only can afford.

123. Man should fervently supplicate the grace of God to imbue him with the spirit of faith, for faith is the basis of the holy law. Man should further implore him for tranquillity, for that is the summit of felicity, tranquillity should be

Mivchar HaPeninim

pursued with avidity in this world, so as to ensure happiness in the world to come - for inexhaustible are the treasures of faith, and unbounded the scope of pious actions.

124. Our industry will not always secure our subsistence, nor will the craftiness of others retard it, for were man even to flee from gain as he flees from death, still gain would overtake him.

125. Irremediable is the folly of him who murmurs against the decrees of his Creator.

Chapter 7

126. To the question, as to what comprises confidence in God, the sage replied, to trust in Him in all thine undertakings.

127. He who submits to the decrees of his Maker with humble resignation, both at their advent and at their close, may justly be termed wise and reliant.

128. Beware, O man, of the thought that thy subsistence is withheld from thee - nor be downcast at the visitation of God.

129. The days of man are pre-ordained and determined. To extend them thine utmost exertions shall not avail, and those decreed to Thee, thy greatest strength will be too feeble to reject.

130. A patient resignation of that which we have once failed to attain affords physical tranquillity, and contentment with that allotted to us by our Creator produces spiritual felicity.

131. The humble committal of our affairs into the hand of God leads to true and pure felicity.

Mivchar HaPeninim

Chapter 8

132. The following laconic observations are said to have been addressed to a king, by one who stood at the gate of the royal palace, but who failed to obtain access.

133.   **1st.** Necessity and hope prompted me to approach thy throne.
2nd. My dire distress admits of no delay.
3rd. My disappointment would gratify the malice of my enemies.
4th. Thine acquiescence would confer advantages, and even thy refusal would relieve me from anxiety and suspense.

134. A supplicant once addressed a prince, to the following effect - I approach thee to solicit that of thee for which I have already supplicated my Creator. Grant it to me, and I shall praise the Lord and thank thee, refuse it, I shall still praise God and excuse thee. This pleased the prince, and he complied with his request.

Mivchar HaPeninim

Chapter 9

135. The sage observes, Brook the truth patiently, however unpalatable it may be.

136. It was asked of the sage to point out when patience is most laudable, He replied, When devoid of ill feelings towards mankind.

137. Patience may be classified under two heads.
> **1st**. That which enables us to endure hardships without repining.
> **2nd**. That which prompts us to abstain from that which the Creator has interdicted.

138. The advantages of memory are twofold.
> **1st**. The recollection of patience under affliction,
> **2nd**. But the most preferable is the remembrance of our Creator, which enables us to remove the barrier between us and Him.

139. O that man would store up patience for misfortune, and gratitude for kindness.

140. Grief for imaginary evil causes actual malady.

Mivchar HaPeninim

141. Care corrodes more than poison.

142. Our grief can only be measured by sensitiveness, and our downfall by our previous eminence.

143. Patience is the safest counsellor, and meekness the truest companion.

144. Sorrow unrestrained by patience prolongs grief.

145. Patience reaps peace, and rashness regret, the former riches, the latter poverty.

146. There are evils which by contrast may be termed felicities.

147. Patience is the invulnerable shield of the defenceless.

148. To the question, who is the most patient, the sage replied, He who curbs his passions.

149. Patience under difficulties dignifies the heart and ensures success.

150. Patience will result in independence, though momentary loss may attend it.

151. He who makes patience his leading

principle, will be led thereby to the realization of his desires.

152. Patience though bitter, yet guards its votaries from injury.

153. Nothing will mitigate our sufferings more than patient endurance.

154. Who is the most esteemed by his Creator, He who is grateful for kindness, resigned in adversity, and praises God.

Mivchar HaPeninim

Chapter 10

155. The sage observes, He who craves more than he needs, mars his actual happiness.

156. The king said to the sage, A mere petition from thee would have inclined me to provide for thee for life.

157. What replied the former, how canst thou expect that one who is richer than thou art should solicit a favour of thee, on being asked for further explanation, he rejoined, Because I am more satisfied with the little, I possess, than thou with thine abundant wealth.

158. He who is satisfied with the portion allotted to him by his Creator may properly be deemed the richest of all mankind.

159. Be content with that which God has bestowed on thee, and envy not the possession of others.

160. Covet not that which was not given to thee, for he who rejoices in his lot will always consider himself abundantly rich.

161. A little will suffice him who only desires from the world that which he actually needs.

Mivchar HaPeninim

162. The smallest gift is acceptable to God from one who is content with the little vouchsafed to him by his Maker.

163. Contentment surpasses intellectuality.

164. Dignity and riches consist in the abandonment of covetousness.

165. He is wise, who seeks from this world but what he requires, for wealth is deceptive, and worldly treasures vanish as speedily as they come.

166. Contentment, which protects its votaries from baseness, is superior to opulence, which exposes its owners to disdain.

167. Contentment of mind surpasses riches.

168. Contentment, with diligence, must lead us not to magnify the possession of others, nor to esteem our own as too scanty, neither to contrast our lot with that above us.

169. The sage recommended to the discontented to recall to their memory their past hardships and vicissitudes, which cannot fail to reconcile them to their comparative present tranquillity - a contrast which admits of no substitute.

Mivchar HaPeninim

170. The fruits of contentment are ease, and those of humility esteem.

171. Regulate thy means, lest thy means will be governed by thy cravings.

172. Contentment is irreconcilable with covetousness.

Mivchar HaPeninim

Chapter 11

173. The sage observes, resignation is the crown of mankind, for avarice is poverty, resignation liberty, and suspense slavery.

174. Regard the world as a blank, and thy share therein as an unexpected prize.

175. The incessant solicitation of favours from mortals betokens lack of faith in God.

Mivchar HaPeninim

Chapter 12

176. Cherish the attribute of diffidence, for it betokens a noble mind.

177. The garb of morality conceals all our feelings.

178. Humility and faith are inseparable and co-existent.

Mivchar   HaPeninim

Chapter 13

179. A cautious tongue ensures prosperity, and adherence to industry averts want.

180. The unwary forfeit esteem.

Chapter 14

181. The sage observed, a good name is the most noble pedigree, and closing the eyes the surest protection against worldly allurements.

182. Care for our reputation confers dignity on the soul, fosters hope of better days and reliance on God, and invests man with perfect faith.

Mivchar HaPeninim

Chapter 15

183. The sage observed, the success of man chiefly depends on his renunciation of worldly pleasures and immoderate desires.

184. The ability to select or reject betokens discrimination, and the government of our passions is the best test of wisdom.

185. Wisdom guides and instructs its adherents, whilst the slave of passions is led astray and perishes.

186. Happy is he who controls his desires, he will once have as a witness Him who exists but is invisible, viz., God, Or, this will secure for him the celestial boon, which is certain though invisible. for no man has ever regretted that which he has resigned in honour of God.

187. We can only approach our Creator by worship. Or, serve God, and we shall assuredly obtain his reward.

188. The fear of God renders our end happier than our beginning. Or, sure to mend his future career.

189. The consciousness of the omniscience and omnipotence of God will guard us from the

Mivchar HaPeninim

commission of evil, this constitutes the reverence of God, and the means of resisting our passions.

190. Misfortune follows the footsteps of the dissipated.

191. The restraint upon our excesses is our safeguard from evil consequences.

192. Fickle words indicate the predominance of the passions.

193. When passions sway reason, it is sure evidence of deep immersion in folly.

194. He who is unable to govern his inclinations and to repress sinful passions, so as to fortify himself against evil consequences, is surely unfit to rule over others.

195. In the absence of reliable counsel, beware not to lean to the dictates of passion, in any object that may engross thine attention, for passion is the enemy of cool deliberation.

196. Prosperous indeed would be the condition of man, but for the following reasons - that the old and experienced are unheeded, that our passions are unbridled, and that our self-love is overweening.

Mivchar HaPeninim

197. Evil imagination and licentiousness corrupt intellect.

198. Good counsel cannot be expected from the fickle, nor concord from the schismatic, nor tranquillity from hope deferred.

199. He who succumbs to his passions will be enslaved, and he who resists them will prevail.

200. He who is a prey to passions entails on himself loss of wealth and honour.

201. The immoderate indulgence of passions will lead man to ignore his Creator, to multiply his sorrow, compunction, and remorse, and to increase his own punishment.

202. Passion may be figuratively termed the twin sister of blindness.

203. Alas, said the sage, that our discretion should slumber whilst our passions are vigilant, hence the submission of the former to the latter.

204. The sages were asked, which is the most commendable war, that which is waged against our evil desires, was their reply.

Chapter 16

205. The sages were asked, what are our duties towards our neighbours, to which they replied, to interpose our good offices, to save them from injury.

206. And what are our duties towards our relatives, to receive them kindly, though they may have repulsed us, and to be generous to them, though they might have been sordid to us.

207. They further observed, Act charitably, both to the deserving and undeserving, for, on the former, thy humanity will be well bestowed, to the latter, thou wilt manifest thy worthiness to carry out the mission of God, who commanded to act kindly and humanely to all.

Chapter 17

208. The sage observes, He cannot be termed wise who reflects after his error, but he deserves that dignity who by circumspection endeavours to avoid it.

209. Intellectual pre-eminence consists in discriminating between the probable and improbable, and being reconciled to the uncontrollable.

210. The wise man disguises not his thoughts, and thus achieves his object.

211. A judicious choice betokens sense, and faith can be established only by reason.

212. It behooves the wise man to study the spirit of the age, to guard his tongue, and to attend to his occupation.

213. Man's writing the combination of his ideas expressed in writing, for no good can be firmly established without it. indicates his knowledge, and the choice of a delegate evinces discriminative power.

214. The reputation of true piety can only be estimated by the standard of acquirements.

Mivchar HaPeninim

215. The ideas of man may be concealed in his writings, but criticism elucidates them.

216. Man's preceptive powers may be recognized by the performance of his occupation, and his disaster by his vocation.

Chapter 18

217. Whatsoever thy origin, said the wise man, endeavour to acquire moral education, for all is valueless without it.

218. He further observed, the fickle-minded has no friend, nor the slave fidelity, nor the covetous rest, nor the avaricious self-respect, nor the impetuous sociability.

219. Who is most certain of success, He who abandons superfluity and follows the shortest road.

220. Good conduct is acquired by experience, moral instruction by the instability of time, and polite manners by those acknowledged as intelligent.

221. The intelligent will never render his presence troublesome, nor intrude upon those who are unwilling to listen to him.

222. The intelligent will not persist in an unwelcome visit, but the fool is insensible to insult.

223. Experience is an unbounded field whereby the wisdom of the intelligent is increased.

Mivchar HaPeninim

224. Cease to address him who turns a deaf ear to thy words.

225. Deign not to address him who interrupts thy discourse, for he lacks good manners.

226. He who cannot control his will, dare not complain if his words are unheeded.

227. He who is deaf to instruction, is doomed to trouble, and ultimately to perish.

228. Instruction, whilst on the one hand it guards from confusion and doubt, will on the other increase the perplexity of the simple-minded, like the day, that lends brightness to sound eyes and blindness to the bat.

229. Never, said the sage, did I occupy a seat that I feared to be required to relinquish for another.

230. A rank too eminent is often the road to degradation.

231. Instruction removes folly, and discretion supports its adherents.

232. Man should adopt the following four principals, -
    1st. To utter words of kindness.

2nd. To devote attention to those with whom he converses.
3rd. To be friendly to his fellow-creatures.
4th. To accustom himself to correct expression - and the following four should be studiously avoided.
1st. To converse with a fool.
2nd. to dispute with the stubborn.
3rd. To natter the undeserving.
4th. To associate with the corrupt.

233. Impart not thy food to the undeserving, viz. converse not with him who is disinclined to listen.

234. Too much gaiety lessens respect.

235. When is it advisable to withhold, rather than to impart instruction, When, replied the sage, it tends rather to enfeeble than to strengthen the intellect, and engenders disrespect towards those who attempt to augment knowledge.

236. A fool is more endurable than half a fool.

237. The Indian sages used to say, Seek not a friend devoid of faith, futurity without good actions, female affection without morality, nor thine own advantage to the injury of others.

Mivchar HaPeninim

238. The most reserved thought cannot escape him who listens with attention, and weighs well the words he chances to hear.

239. Self-denial will command the respect of the intellectual.

240. Confide in the discreet and generous, associate - but with caution - with the erudite, though avaricious, that thou mayest reap the advantage of his learning, court the philanthropist, though unlearned, and reciprocate his generosity by thy knowledge, Or, that a reciprocal benefit may result. but shun the sordid fool.

Mivchar HaPeninim

Chapter 19

241. The sage observed, good conduct and good manners are the stepping-stones to a high rank, and lead to the practice of kindness and piety.

242. The following lines were addressed by Aristotle to his royal disciple, Alexander the Macedonian, govern thy subjects with kindness, and thus thou wilt gain then-affections. Mild and lenient government is more durable by far than compulsory submission, for what boots the possession of the body, without that of the heart. Affection gained by kindness insures allegiance.

243. For the whisper of rebellion is the sure precursor of its fulfilment, endeavour therefore to silence murmur, and rebellion will be stifled.

244. In your demeanour be affable and courteous towards the noble-minded, but severe and rigorous towards the wicked, for whilst respect and courtesy must improve the former, rigour alone will reclaim the latter.

Mivchar HaPeninim

Chapter 20

245. The sage observed, the short - comings of the uniformly just and faithful should readily be pardoned.

246. He used to say, an evil associate seeks occasion to cavil, and disdains apology.

247. A man asked the sage to advise him with whom to associate, to which he replied, this is a question to which I can offer no solution.

248. There is some utility in every friendship, save in that of the simple-minded.

249. The conduct, like the advice, of a true friend is based on good faith, such a friend will assist our intellect, but not flatter our passions.

250. I am more in thine power, said one to his friend, than thy own hand, and more submissive than thine own slave.

251. The following three things are due to our friends - our undivided attention when they enter our house, our welcome when they sit therein, and our ear when they speak.

252. The seducer is brother to the murderer, and silence the sister of complaisance.

253. My son, said the sage, never exchange an old friend for a new one, whilst the heart of the first remains true to thee - deem one enemy not insignificant, nor a thousand friends superabundant.

254. Transient are the treasures and possessions of the world, the most lasting is morality, and the securest stronghold, friendship, increase therefore, the former, and seek safety in the latter.

255. The friendless man is as the left hand without a right one.

256. The death of a friend is equivalent to the loss of a limb.

257. He may be termed a true friend, who never misleads thee, who promotes thine advantage, to his own detriment, and who is anxious to deliver thee from oppression.

258. It was asked of the wise man, whom he loved most, his brother or his friend, to which he replied, I never love a brother unless he is my friend.

259. Three things are calculated to retain the unmixed esteem of our friends –

Mivchar HaPeninim

1st. To anticipate them in our salutations.

2nd. To show them due respect in society.

3rd. And to designate them by their endearing appellation.

260. There are three degrees of folly - to censure actions from which we are not exempt, to discover faults in others, which we are prone to overlook in ourselves, and to solicit a useless favour. A favour which can be dispensed with.

261. There are likewise three degrees of friendship - The first, like our sustenance, is indispensable to our existence, the second may be regarded in the light of an occasional, but necessary remedy, and the third may be compared to a distemper, which should be carefully guarded against.

262. The wise man said to his son, in thy intercourse with mankind, endeavour to cultivate the society of him whose friendship will ennoble thee, whose reverence will react on thee, who will aid thee in need, who will correct thy expressions, who will bear with thy failings, who will never lead thee into mishaps, and whose example will never corrupt thee.

263. Friends may be classified under three heads.

1st. He who devotes his heart and means to thy support - value him as a faithful friend.

2nd. He who would extort from thee every advantage, and sacrifice thee from the merest selfishness - him number amongst the faithless.

3rd. He whose friendship consists in mere words, and who is ever ready to extort more than he will confer - on such friendship do not rely.

264. The friendship of the noble-minded is an inestimable treasure, but that of the worthless, is ever attended with regret.

265. Knowledge is our true friend, but passions are our enemies.

266. The friendship of the ignorant is dangerous, their aversion cheering.

267. Affability strengthens love, but sullenness strips intercourse of its cordiality.

Chapter 21

268. The sage observes, the most docile animal needs the rod, the most chaste female a husband, and the wisest of men counsel.

Chapter 22

269. The sage observes, If thy friend wrong thee, chide him privately, if he heed thee, thine object is attained, if not, reprimand him before one or two, should he remain deaf to thy remonstrance, cast him off as an encumbrance.

270. Admonition profits not him who lacks an inherent moral sense.

271. Remonstrate ere you punish.

Mivchar HaPeninim

Chapter 23

272. Associate only with such as value their position, for there is no solace in those who are regardless of self-respect.

273. Agreeable intercourse and uninterrupted friendship are the results of an exalted mind, graced with urbanity.

274. Good companionship protects from evil.

Chapter 24

275. Netek, [scall] said the sage, did I argue with him whom I found blind to my failings.

276. He used to say, Better is he who privately discloses to me my faults, than the gift of many golden coins from an over indulgent friend.

277. He used to say, I prize him who privately points out my errors.

Mivchar HaPeninim

Chapter 25

278. The sage observed, true friendship, with good counsel, demands both our pure esteem and implicit confidence.

279. As the roots firmly fixed in the heart exhibit their branches on the tongue, so will perfect love only emanate from a true heart.

280. The sage was asked to define love, and replied, The tendency of hearts, and their mutual inclination.

281. He used to say, the space of a needle's eye suffices for two friends, whilst the universe itself can scarcely contain two enemies.

282. To distinguish thy friend from thine enemy, examine thine own heart.

283. Rely not on him who burthens thee with his sorrows, but withholds from thee his joys.

284. The sage was asked, whom he loved most, either him, he said, who has experienced the greatest kindness from me, or I from him.

285. We may recognize the friend when our heart is cognizant of his affections, and our tongue utters his praise.

286. Flatter not thy friend, nor inquire too anxiously after him, lest thou tempt his enemy to gainsay thee, and seek to sever thee from him.

287. Be liberal to thy friends with thy heart and thy means, to thy acquaintances with thine influence and kind words, bestow on mankind thy countenance and friendly salutation, on thine enemies, thy charity - be mindful of the law of God, but of thy reputation above all.

288. Beware of those who measure their love by their interest, for the one expires when the other is attained.

289. Depend not on the favour of the prince, if the minister frown on thee, but with the favour of the latter thou neediest not despair of the former.

290. I never failed to repay the love of my friends with pure and undivided affections, nor to pray to God to restore mine enemies to the path of rectitude, neither betrayed the secret entrusted to me, nor desired a thing unworthy of me, nor did I assent and retract, even at the risk of my worldly treasures.

291. Patience is always commendable, save when our friend is calumniated.

Chapter 26

292. Let animosity vanish on the appearance of the excuse.

293. It is ungenerous to chide him who craves our pardon, and to harbour resentment against him who apologizes.

294. Avoid the friendship of those who will neither forgive, nor accept an apology.

295. Let reconciliation crown the apology and confession, however laconic, for forgiveness is the attribute of the philanthropist.

296. The following reply was made by a friend to whom an apologetic appeal was addressed - Thy Creator never demanded from thee this justification, neither do my favourable sentiments and disinterested love for thee admit the very least idea of malice.

297. Man should remember grievances only until some justification is offered, though the first may be certain and the second doubtful, so that the aggrieved may retain some influence over him for a fitting opportunity.

298. Who may be denominated the indolent amongst mankind, He who neglects to gain

Mivchar HaPeninim

friends, but the greatest sluggard of all is he who possessed friends, but neglected to retain them.

299. Reject no justification from whomsoever it may emanate, regard not whether it be sincere or feigned, for he who appeases thee publicly esteems thee highly, and he who intrigues against thee secretly still respects thee.

Chapter 27

300. Beware of acquaintances from whom thou canst learn no good.

301. Intercourse with worthless associates engenders evil manners.

302. The sage was asked, how can a discreet man test his own temper, to which he replied, By the patient endurance of a bad wife.

303. A bad wife may be compared to a wolf, that changes its coat, but not its nature.

304. The most dangerous alliance is consorting with a bad woman - that is indeed a deep wound.

305. Avoid the companionship of the arrogant, for often has it contaminated the meek and unassuming.

306. He used to say, let thine intercourse be with the noble and liberal-minded, for both the honour and disgrace of man are the natural results of his associates.

307. He who enters on evil designs will be suspected.

Mivchar HaPeninim

308. He who has incurred suspicion, dares not complain of harsh criticism.

309. Associate with the wise, listen to their sayings, and depart not from them.

310. What is most advantageous to man, The sage replied, Either the possession of good sense, or worldly means that are productive of respect, a wife that will screen his faults, or silence that will hide his failings, - but better the grave than the absence of all these.

311. They used to say, four propensities destroy mankind - pride, waywardness, indolence, and rashness.

Chapter 28

312. The sage has said, He alone is a true friend, who will serve thee with his means in time of distress, and with his soul in time of need and danger.

313. In thy choice of a friend, try to provoke him, if, in the heat of passion, he admits the truth, welcome him as thy friend, if not, discard him.

314. Rely not on gratitude until thou hast tested it by refusal, for the truly grateful is patient, whilst the sullen is thankless indeed.

Chapter 29

315. The sage has said, disclose not that to thy friend which thou wouldst conceal from thine enemy.

316. There was a man who, after confiding a secret to his friend, asked him if he understood him. Yes, replied the other, but I have since forgotten it.

317. He was asked, how to conceal a secret effectually. Said he, I make my heart its tomb.

318. The sage was asked the surest means of keeping a secret. His reply was, I chide the narrator and hide the narration.

319. I never, said the sage, condemned the betrayer of my entrusted secret, but reproached mine own heart, which was too narrow to retain it, and led me to deposit it in his.

320. A narrow mind has a broad tongue.

321. He used to say, an unrevealed secret is thy captive, but disclosed it is thy captor.

322. That only is a secret which lies between two, with three it ceases to be so.

Chapter 30

323. The sage observes, we submit involuntarily to him who has chosen righteousness for his stronghold.

324. Righteousness adopted as a standard, becomes an impregnable shield.

325. Faithfulness is the offspring of benevolence.

326. The vow of the philanthropist is promptly fulfilled, that of the avaricious is tardy and evasive.

327. If thou wouldst avoid repentance, give thy denial rather than thine assent, but thine assent once given, endure it to injury, but retract not, for **No** that follows **Yes** is culpable indeed.

Chapter 31

328. The sage was asked, what constitutes modesty, He answered, the blush caused by the consciousness of our secret misdeeds.

329. He was further asked, what constitutes liberality, The due estimation of that which is lawful, and the application of our means to our moral obligations.

330. What constitutes humility, Meekness united with wisdom.

331. Being asked for further explanation, he replied, Humility, accompanied by the observance of the Divine law, an upright conduct, order in domestic expenditure, and calm submission to the vicissitudes of life.

332. What is piety, to avoid in secret that for which we should blush in public.

333. Refrain from sins, for true piety exists but with spotless and pure morality, and is heightened by a judicious dispensation of our wealth.

334. True religion is incompatible with simulated piety; true piety consists in self-abnegation.

335. He used to say, the generous and noble-hearted only can lay claim to true virtue.

336. The first step to unobtrusive piety, is to afford a kind reception to our friends, the second, to manifest our friendship to them, the third, to comply - if possible - with their wishes, and the fourth, to participate in their adversity.

Mivchar HaPeninim

Chapter 32

337. The sage observes, my words may occasion regret, but my silence will avoid it.

338. He continued, Words uttered are my masters, but words suppressed, I am theirs.

339. The injury caused by silence is easier repaired than that caused by speech.

340. He used to say, what boot words, which if attributed to me might tend to my injury, and which if withheld would not benefit me.

341. Many advantages have been forfeited by an untimely word.

342. Sorrow occasioned by silence is less insupportable than that caused by words, nay, even death from taciturnity is preferable to death from loquacity.

343. The most acceptable devotion consists in silence and hope.

344. Silence may be accompanied with one regret, speech with many.

345. Silence is preferable to an untimely word.

346. Silence increases respect and reverence.

347. Be as sparing with thy tongue, as thou art with thy wealth.

348. In the absence of a moral instructor, adhere to silence.

349. The destroyer of man lurks under his tongue, and death resides between his cheeks.

350. The preponderance of words over intellect may result in persuasiveness, that of intellect over words may entail blame, but beautiful is it when the one graces the other.

351. Words that exceed discretion acquire the ascendency over us, but when discretion prevails over our words, we govern them.

352. A certain Arab, having joined a circle of friends, listened patiently to them, with profound silence. He was at length asked, whence your rank amongst the noble and accomplished of Arabia, He replied meekly, my friends, the properties of the ear are man's alone, but those of the tongue belong to his fellow-men.

353. A certain sage, renowned for his reservedness, caution, and eloquence, was asked to define the nature of speech, its

Mivchar HaPeninim

advantages and disadvantages. My friends, replied he, speech may be classified under four heads.

> **1st**. Words which may promise momentary benefit, but may still have in their train fatal consequences, to avoid which is advantageous.
>
> **2nd**. Words which hold out no advantage, and may yet be pregnant with injurious results, these are indeed extremely dangerous.
>
> **3rd**. Words that promise neither advantage nor disadvantage, the avoidance of which would afford both physical and mental ease.
>
> **4th**. Words which may promise benefit and security for the future, these constitute the spirit of conversation. Reject the three, and embrace the fourth.

354. The sage observes, be sparing in thy words, for the less thy words the less thine errors.

355. In thy conversation by night, let thy voice be subdued, and by day cast thine eyes around thee ere thou speakers.

356. Impart thy secret in a plain, and thy advice on the summit of mountains, so that thy view may be unimpeded.

Mivchar HaPeninim

357. He was wont to say, A slip of the tongue is more dangerous than the slip of the foot, for the slip of the tongue may cost thy head, whilst the slip of the foot may easily be cured.

Chapter 33

358. The sage observes, A truthful word is better than silence.

359. Some individuals having in the presence of the king indiscriminately censured speech, were thus addressed by him - Ear be it from me to agree with you, for he who knows when to speak, will likewise know when to be silent.

360. None but the profound scholar or distinguished orator should address an assembly.

361. There are many persuasive words that may soften down resentment.

Chapter 34

362. The sage observed, He who is cited to appear before the king feels the extent of the whole realm a dungeon.

363. He used to say, give due reverence to God, obedience to the king, and let your conduct towards your fellow-men be affable.

364. The king and the law are twins; the one is indispensable to the other.

365. The sage continued, Dwell not in a city which lacks a venerated king, a righteous judge, a skilful physician, an established market, and a navigable river.

366. A king may be compared to a fire—at too great a distance we feel its want, when too nigh we scorch.

367. If the king is opposed to thee, restrain thy words, for thou wilt surely be vanquished.

368. The most worthless part of wealth is that which is unemployed, the most worthless of companions is the seducer, the most worthless of kings is he whom the innocent dread, and the most worthless country is that which, though fertile. Or, which affords neither fertility nor safety. yet affords its inhabitants no safety.

369. A righteous king is more advantageous to his subjects than the most fruitful season.

370. The friendship of a king, though it confers dignity and honour, is like a lofty and steep mountain, abounding in delicious and refreshing fruits, but overrun with ferocious beasts - its ascent is toilsome, and the dwelling thereon doubly so.

371. Against the injustice of our fellow-men we appeal to the king, but against that of the king where is our redress,

Chapter 35

372. The sage observes, the wise find tranquillity in discovering the truth, the ignorant in folly.

373. Truth establishes all things, falsehood overthrows them.

374. A despot once condemned to death a sage, on false accusation. When led to death, he perceived his wife weeping bitterly. Why weepiest thou, said the sage. Have I not caused for tears, replied the wife, seeing that thou sufferers' death innocently, well, replied the sage, calmly, wouldst thou see me die guilty.

Chapter 36

375. The sage observes, the wisdom of the poor is often despised, but riches cover folly.

376. He further observed, the wealth of a man conceals his failings, and justifies perfidy, but the intelligence of the poor is contemned, and his wisdom is counted as folly.

Mivchar HaPeninim

Chapter 37

377. The sage said, the ignorant glory in sordidness, and disdain wisdom and morality, but the wise glory in morality and wisdom, and disdain sordidness and folly.

378. It is related, that a rich man, sumptuously attired, happened to pass a sage who was meanly clad. Well, exclaimed the former, is it thou who hast written on science, philosophy, and politics, yes, mildly replied the sage, but the standard of true wisdom is not measured by costly raiment, but by pure and genuine knowledge.

Mivchar HaPeninim

Chapter 38

379. The sage says, the attributes of polite manners are in ten.
> **1st.** Utterance of truth.
> **2nd.** Love of mankind.
> **3rd.** Liberality to the supplicant.
> **4th.** Gratitude.
> **5th.** Affability.
> **6th.** Faithfulness.
> **7th.** Condescension to our fellow-man.
> **8th.** Courtesy to friends.
> **9th.** Hospitality.
> **10th.** Modesty surpasses all.

380. The sage said, Wise though thou be, adhere to these pleasant attributes, and they will afford thee solace here and hereafter, be forgiving to those who have wronged thee, instruct others in the way of kindness, and shun the ignorant.

381. He continued, Agreeable manners, may be enumerated thus.
> **1st.** The fear of God.
> **2nd.** Honour to fellow beings.
> **3rd.** Contentedness.
> **4th.** Patience.
> **5th.** Gratitude.
> **6th.** Diffidence.
> **7th.** Liberality.

Mivchar HaPeninim

8th. Self-government.
9th. Emulation.
10th. Modesty.
11th. Utterance of truth.
12th. Faithfulness.
13th. and Cheerfulness.

382. He observed, Urbanity may be further reduced to the following seven heads.
1st. Affability.
2nd. Humility.
3rd. Esteem to relatives.
4th. Impartiality in self judgment, irrespective of our peculiar emotions.
5th. A due sense of decorum.
6th. Forgiveness under provocation.
7th. and Self-command.

383. He continued, He who possesses those qualities is sure to enjoy an unruffled existence, both in this world and in that which is to come.

384. Perfect diffidence consists in the seven following qualifications.
1st. Gentleness of expression.
2nd. Disinterestedness.
3rd. The eschewing of injury.
4th. Solicitude for our self-respect.
5th. The avoidance of calumny.
6th. Faithfulness.
7th. and Secrecy.

Mivchar HaPeninim

385. The philanthropist will earn superiority - the selfish slight.

386. A certain philanthropist, in an interview with a king, was asked to recount some of his generous deeds. He meekly replied, I would rather your liege should hear it from others, than from me.

387. But, replied the king, I command thee to speak. Well, said the other, never did I assume an attitude of superiority before my fellow-men. How so asked the king, because said he, that Or, I would not willingly parade. it shall not be supposed that I parade my rank, exalted station, and benevolence, although I may excel in these points.

388. Neither have I retaliated an injury, for, alleged he, if the aggressor be a man of estimation, his motives are no doubt unquestionable, and claim my forbearance, if the contrary, I would not subject myself to the censure of the worthless.

389. Nor did my gifts to my fellow-man ever bring the blush of shame into his countenance, though at the cost of my worldly possessions. Well, quota the king, thou, indeed, art fitted to rule over thine own people and others.

390. He used to observe, He cannot be termed

Mivchar HaPeninim

munificent who returns liberality for liberality, and hospitality for hospitality - such is merely a requital, but he is truly munificent who returns liberality for selfishness, and kindness for repulsiveness.

391. He whom the Creator has favoured with the following four qualifications will endure unscathed the privations of this world.
>**1st**. An easy mind.
>**2nd**. Regularity in diet.
>**3rd**. Veracity.
>**4th**. and Faithfulness.

392. Falsehood and humility are incompatible.

393. It has often been remarked, that a benign disposition, a kind neighbour, a comely dwelling, and clean garments, ensure a long and happy existence.

394. He who is blessed by the Creator with a benevolent disposition will partake of future bliss.

395. What constitutes the most noble pedigree, Disinterestedness was his reply.

396. He was wont to remark, the outset, like the termination, of a cheerful mind is felicitous, its commencement is wisdom, and its end is peace, for a felicitous life and perpetual bliss

Mivchar HaPeninim

awaits the tranquil mind, nor can the vicissitudes of the world affect him.

397. A certain emir was asked by what means he had attained dominion over his people. He replied, By the unlimited practice of hospitality, by dismissing the sycophant, and by succouring the needy.

398. Alas, exclaimed the sage, that a man should purchase slaves with wealth, and neglect to gain free men by his kindness.

399. A strict adherence to the following five principles constitutes a sure and constant safeguard.
        1st. To avoid the infliction of injury.
        2nd. To possess a tranquil mind.
        3rd. To renounce flatterers.
        4th. To adopt good morals.
        5th. And to practise benevolence.

400. The most eminent man is he whose mildness and sociability surpass those of others.

Chapter 39

401. The sage observes, the neglect of friendly intercourse entails a loss on ourselves. A troublesome visitor will meet with scorn and reproach.

402. Rare and far between visits increase love.

403. He used to remark, Frequent visits engender dislike, if rare they tend to increase friendship.

404. Let the distance of a mile not deter thee from visiting the sick, two from establishing peace between fellow-creatures, nor three from paying homage to thy Creator.

405. Beware of frequent visits, for they often produce alienation, like showers, whose frequent descent annoys, but whose timely advent is devoutly prayed for.

Chapter 40

406. A Troublesome guest is more intolerable to the patient than the disease itself.

407. A patient annoyed by the lengthy visit of an unwelcome guest, addressed him in the following laconic and ironical strain. Dost, thou claim any thing in my house, or do I owe aught to thee, if so, take it and be gone.

408. It is further related of a patient, who was asked to state his grievance, my numerous sins, said he.

409. What is thy desire, Forgiveness, he replied. Shall we call in a physician, it was he, replied the patient, who caused my illness.

Chapter 41

410. The sage observed, there are two blessings which are the rarest in the world, and which become daily still rarer, legitimate means applied to pious purposes, and a trusty friend to rely on.

411. A man asked the sage to advise him with whom to associate. The sage replied this is a question, to which I can offer no solution.

Mivchar HaPeninim

Chapter 42

412. The sage thus addressed his son - Peace be with thee, my son. Ponder on this mine epistle, and direct thine heart to my good counsel, despise not mine instructions, and incline thine ear to my words.

413. Practise that which I have written, thou wilt then succeed and prosper, and let naught else occupy thy mind, nor engross thine attention.

414. Know then, that wisdom is based on study, study on reflection, perseverance, and diligence, for blindness is not of the eyes, but of the heart.

415. Therefore reflect on mine epistle and on its contents, for what availed the open eye, if the heart be blind and obdurate, Or, what gain is there, if the ear listens and is attentive, or what boots the beauty of external appearance, if the heart be void of understanding,

416. Has not the sage often declared that vision is dimmed, if the heart be blind, many there are whose appearance may influence thee, but listen to their words, and thou wilt number them amongst the dumb.

417. Again, He who would correct the untoward and instruct the grossly ignorant resembles him who would play music to the dead or invoke idols.

418. But the least admonition suffices for the intelligent, a word will impress him with the important duties which wisdom enjoins, and will teach him to infer, to weigh, and to compare,

419. Experience will make him wise, enlarge his mind, and reveal to him, that which was concealed.

420. For, as it was observed by a sage to his son, know that morality is the summit of discretion, and silence the crown of wisdom.

421. The pursuit of wisdom leads to happiness and to the protection of friendship, whilst in the train of folly follow misery and hatred.

422. Forgiveness yields felicity, faithfulness is the ornament of mankind, and uprightness the best of associates.

423. Wisdom is a goodly inheritance, falsehood is the key to guilt, hypocrisy causes evil and encircles with hatred.

Mivchar   HaPeninim

424. Anger perplexes the pleader, forwardness enfeebles counsel, feeble counsel deteriorates morals, the deterioration of morals engenders disgrace and promotes strife.

425. Excessive laughter denotes folly, and he who exposes his teeth lessens his respect.

426. The reign of falsehood is but brief.

427. Questionable resorts excite suspicion, evil associates destroy religious principles, but the society of the virtuous increase's intelligence, exhilarates the heart, sustains knowledge, brightens the countenance, and is the herald of virtue.

428. Morality develops the acumen of the discreet, hut the intelligent often subject themselves to contempt from the want of morality, for intellect without morality is utterly useless, whilst their union tends to enhance station, distinction, and diligence.

429. Were it not for morality, there would have been no distinction between man and man, but good morals confer pre-eminence.

430. Know further, my son, that there is no remedy for folly, for it is an incurable disease.

431. The discreet reflects glory and blessing on

Mivchar HaPeninim

himself, honour on his house, is an ornament to his friends, a credit to his kindred, and knows when to assume dignity or meekness.

432. The intelligent, however humble, will find ready access to the presence of kings, be seated with the great, introduced amongst princes, mankind will praise him, his acquaintance will be coveted, his friendship valued, his enmity dreaded, and he will remain his own monitor and guide.

433. The wise man is his own best monitor, but the most useful moral guide to the untutored is the learned.

434. The intelligent and experienced are the fittest guides, and none deserves implicit friendship more than a benevolent disposition.

435. The wise of heart may be termed acute and penetrating. Man learns in order to attain knowledge, time confers experience and enlightenment, but morality without intelligence is unproductive.

436. To ascertain a character, learn his companion, for man imitates his associates, therefore, in all thy relations, join the virtuous and shun the wicked, lest thou be contaminated.

437. Know further, my son, that the presence of the ignorant will never be regarded, his absence regretted, nor will he ever acquire respect.

438. In the assembly of the wise he will hear and see that which he can neither understand nor appreciate.

439. Take heed, my son, that wisdom be ever present before thee, slight it not, beware of coarse expressions in society, avoid loquacity in the presence of the wise in the holy law, and frivolity before the learned men.

440. Hearken to the learned in the holy law, be submissive to the wise, respect the great, be condescending to the lowly, and abandon hypocrisy and pride, for they are injurious to mankind and are akin to madness and levity.

441. Be aware, my son, that the characteristic of the liberal and noble-minded is, to love mankind, to overlook their faults, to bear no grudge to those who offend him, to pardon injuries, to be affable to the poor, and devoted to his friends.

442. My son, intermeddle not with the affairs of others, nor pry into their concerns, reflect well on my injunction, and the Eternal will assist thee.

Chapter 43

443. The sage addressed his son - Consent not to rule over thy townsmen, nor despise trifles, for they may become of importance.

444. Contend not with the passionate man, lest thou vex him, nor admit into thy society those who dispute merely to oppose, rejoice not at the fall of thine enemies, for thou knowest not what may befall thee.

445. Evince not thy superiority, though thou hast power to exercise it, for alas! thou knowest not what time has in store for thee.

446. Deride not the errors of thy fellow-man, for thou canst scarcely control the words of thine own mouth, and be to the utmost lenient to the faults of others.

447. Confer not hastily thy friendship, let truth be ever before thee, thus thou wilt be safe and unshackled all thy days.

448. The sage continued, know that the fear of God and the observance of his commandments constitute the summit of faith.

449. Reflect that God ordains the elevation of the lowly and the humbling of the great,

Mivchar HaPeninim

therefore, humble thyself, in order that God may exalt thee.

450. Delay not repentance, for death comes unawares.

451. Increase the number of thy friends, and set not thine heart against him who wronged thee.

452. Barter not thy wife for the charms of another, for lust deludes the intellect and alas! it misled one who was wiser than thou art.

453. Deem thyself poor, though thou art rich, for thou wilt once be separated from riches.

454. Stand not before the king, when he is in anger, nor before a river when it is overflowing.

455. Decide not without mature and trustworthy counsel, dread the wicked or, be mindful not to forfeit the regard of the good. and be wary of their favours.

456. My son, seek to acquire a good wife and a kind friend, the one brings thee tranquillity within, and the other without.

457. There is no greater riches than health, no greater pleasure than a cheerful heart.

458. God gives to despots power over the

wealth of those whose hands are shut against the poor.

459. Magnanimity may be defined, as the due appreciation of benevolent sentiments, combined with a submission to the hidden decrees of Providence, or, not to betray intrusted secrets. secrecy in the performance of good action.

460. Human affairs may be considered from three points of view.
> **1st**. Such as are obviously good.
> **2nd**. Such as are overtly bad.
> **3rd**. Such as are doubtful. Adhere to the first, dismiss the second, and in the third cast thy burthen on God.

461. The sage saith, exclude not wholly the name of God from thy speech, lest thine heart become obdurate, for the obdurate heart is distant from God.

462. Censure not the faults of others on the assumption of superiority, lest you be unmindful of your own faults.

463. The sage was want to observe, He who is exempt from the following three errors will never lack three advantages.
> **1st**. He who is free from anger will obtain esteem.

2nd. He who is pure from transgressions will gain honour.

3rd. He who is free from avarice will earn dignity.

464. Ingratitude is wickedness, and the society of the ignorant a sore disease.

465. He used to say, He was never ensnared who knew his own position, nor has regret ever followed the closing of the eyes against evil.

466. The morals of man depend on the dictates of his heart; hence his demeanour and disposition are formed by his counsel and intellect. The characteristics of man are the reflex of his heart; hence they are recognized by his counsel and intellect.

467. He who overrates the worth of mankind has an erroneous conception of the world.

468. The neglectful is past remedy.

469. Wisdom can never be termed perfect in man, unless attended by intellect, meekness, and reverence for God, unless it rejects flattery, forwardness, and pertinacity, and is exempt from covetousness, lust, and falsehood, for he who covets will also lie in wait, and he who is addicted to lust is sure to err, and the liar will forfeit all faith and ever incur suspicion, and, lastly, it must be based on clemency, silence, and deliberation.

470. The sage observes, He who avoids rashness, perverseness, and indolence will escape their four evil consequences, for the result of rashness is regret, that of perverseness audacity, the end of pride hatred, and that of indolence ruin.

471. God will raise the renown of him who purifies his heart from secret errors, and establish the temporal and spiritual happiness of him who is solicitous for his own future welfare, and he who seeks to be reconciled to God, will by the help of his Maker be reconciled to his fellow-men.

472. The sage observes, the practice of the following three things will never weary - According to another reading, Will never be ascribed to sinister motives.
    1st. Good morals.
    2nd. The avoidance of inflicting injury.
    3rd. To keep from transgression.

473. The sage addressed his son - My son, reserve thy coin for charity, thy provision to feed the hungry, and thy knowledge of the law for the appointed day.

474. As thou should dread the society of the

simpleton, so thou mayest rest secure in that of the wise.

475. He who tolerates the society of the liar is worse than he, for his words are unquestioned by the godless, but the god-fearing will ponder on them.

476. He who shuns falsehood will control his tongue and diminish his failings.

477. Undeserved encomiums should produce sorrow rather than joy.

478. He who shuns sinners will escape degradation.

479. A trustworthy stranger is preferable to a deceitful relative.

480. Habit governs all things, sound conclusion can be attained only by consultation, and happiness perpetuated by kindness seasonably performed.

481. The public avowal of error will ensure praise in private, and he who conceals not his faults will consign them to oblivion.

482. Be certain, that he who attributes to thee merit that is not thine is unworthy of reliance.

483. An ungodly meeting is sure to result in an ungodly separation.

484. The simpleton is wont to bestow praise where censure is obviously due.

485. He who possesses the following three qualities may be said to be fully entitled to the claim to truthfulness.

> **1st.** That temptation will never lead him to falsehood.
> **2nd.** That anger will not prompt him to prevaricate.
> **3rd.** That power will never induce him to lay hand on that which is not his.

486. These two are essentially incompatible, - an easy mind and avarice.

487. The following six cannot escape vexation.

> **1st.** The wealthy reduced to poverty.
> **2nd.** The affluent anxious for his wealth.
> **3rd.** The vindictive.
> **4th.** The covetous.
> **5th.** The aspirant to unmerited rank.
> **6th.** The immoral in companionship with moral men.

488. Three persons claim our utmost compassion.

> **1st.** The learned controlled by the infatuated Eccentric.

2nd. The righteous ruled by the wicked.
3rd. and the noble-minded dependent on the worthless.

489. It was related of one who publicly remonstrated with his friend, exclaiming, I was told thou didst make me the object of thy slander. Alas! replied the other, that the association with the wicked should occasion the calumniation of the virtuous.

490. Three characters can best be judged by three tests.

1st. The meek in anger.
2nd. The hero in battle.
3rd. The friend in need.

491. There was a king who commanded the execution of one of his ministers, on whose girdle was the following inscription - Since the decree of God is irrevocable, the efforts of men are vain, since treachery is inherent in nature, reliance on untried friends is idle, and since death waylays mankind, the trust in this world is mere madness. In the original the sentence is in the conditional.

492. The sage observes, Poverty and hunger are more endurable than over-exertion caused by the cravings of an insatiable disposition, no wealth can surpass contentment, no intellect is equivalent to good demeanour, and no charms can be compared to an affable mind.

493. Answer not the fool in his error, for thine attempt to instruct him will rouse his hatred.

494. I dread to wrong those, said the sage, whose sole advocate is God.

495. Inure thy soul to shun error, thus shalt thou be termed wise, thine instruction will be obeyed, mankind will imitate thee, and profit by thine example.

496. He is invulnerable to all mundane privation, in whom are combined piety and rectitude.

Mivchar HaPeninim

Chapter 44

497. The sage observes, Man should relinquish the allurements of this world for the love of God, for they incite man to rebel, and their abandonment alone brings man nearer to his Creator.

498. Man's chief aim in this world is the acquisition of riches, pleasure, and honour, but ardently as he may pursue them, they will elude his grasp, whilst he who abjures them and needs not the help of mortals will be esteemed, he is rich, for he rejoices in his lot, he enjoys tranquillity, for he has banished worldly care, and he attains his desire without anxiety and exertion.

499. The wise man rejoices not in his abundant in the original the sentence is in the conditional. wealth, nor sorrows at his humble lot, but he will exult in his intellect and in his former good deeds, of which none can deprive him, nor will he ever be held amenable for any omission. Or, nor will his conduct make him responsible for the deeds of another, viz., caused by his example.

500. The sage was wont to say, seek after that which thou needest, and abandon that which thou needest not, for in abandoning that which

Mivchar HaPeninim

thou needest not, thou art sure to gain that which thou needest.

501. He who loves life must practise meekness.

502. O that man, exclaimed the sage, would in prosperity reflect on reverses, and in sorrow on hope! he would perpetuate happiness and escape sin.

503. He who is not resigned to the decrees of the Creator will be discontented with the course of this world, he who would reduce God's mercy to the mere relief of physical necessities displays gross ignorance, and he who envies the possession of another prolongs his own grief, and his morbid Ness is past cure.

504. How superior, exclaimed the sage, is poverty to riches! for, said he, never did the desire for poverty lead man to rebel, whilst the craving after riches often tempts him to do so.

505. Dissatisfaction at the vicissitudes of life arises chiefly from the following four tendencies.
> **1st**. The poor in vain pursuit after riches.
> **2nd**. Endless care.
> **3rd**. Overwhelming anxiety.
> **4th**. Wishes unfulfilled.

506. He who duly values his own dignity will

hold the world in little estimation.

507. Who is the most dignified amongst men, He who can behold without envy the worldly possessions of another.

508. To the question, what lends a charm to life and banishes sadness, the sage replied, A due estimation of the duties we owe to the world, and of those which the world owes to us, as the adage says, the world honours him most who disregards its vanities, and slights him who courts them, for the end of riches may be poverty, the result of rank degradation, and the consequences of ease disease.

509. Man resembles the fruit of the tree, which though it escapes injury during its growth, yet must decay at maturity.

510. Man can likewise be compared to one encompassed by ferocious animals and lurking enemies, and though he may elude some, he cannot escape all, he who views the world thus will not be elated at the happiness it confers, nor dejected by the mishaps it inflicts, as the sage observes, this world is fraught with grief, and its few joys should be regarded as gain unlooked for.

511. Who may be deemed truly pious, He who

Mivchar HaPeninim

willingly resigns mundane advantages, in the hope of future felicity.

512. He was wont to observe, regard this world, as though thou wert destined to live forever, and the world to come as though thou wert to die to-morrow.

513. The following two good qualities are unsurpassable, labour whose object is not of this world, and condescension without meanness.

514. Humility leads to dignity, piety is often crowned with honour, and contentment with riches.

515. The sage thus addressed his friends, look upon death with indifference, for its bitterness is commensurate with its fear.

516. Truth and justice are balm to the soul, and the indulgence in sensuality its bane.

517. He was wont to teach, be prepared to die with resignation, so shalt thou enjoy life undisturbedly.

518. Man may approach his end resignedly or reluctantly, but he who deadens his passions renders his death everlasting life.

Mivchar HaPeninim

519. He who would benefit his soul must be indifferent to transient possessions.

520. The love of worldly possessions is a source of grief, lesson the one, and thou wilt diminish the other.

521. It is preferable to sympathize with the unhappy, then to rejoice with the mirthful.

522. Man in pursuit of worldly gain may be compared to a thirsty man within reach of briny waters, the more he drinks, the more is his thirst increased.

523. Man may also be compared to a famished dog, gnawing a dry bone, until the blood streams from its month, whilst, under the false impression of imbibing nourishment, it greedily licks its own blood. Thus, it is with man engaged solely with worldly pursuits, and regardless of the service of his Creator, believing himself a gainer, whilst he is really a loser, for man is responsible for his deed's hereafter.

524. He who pines not after that which he failed to obtain insures a tranquil life, an undisturbed intellect, and long days.

525. Our principal griefs result from love of this world.

526. To repine at the events of life, is to rebel against God.

527. The sage was once requested to impart a salutary lesson, to which he replied, be not elated at that which the world bestows, nor dejected at that which it denies, but exult at that which thou hast well performed, and regret that which thou hast neglected, and fear a hereafter.

528. He observed, Let the dread of repentance be thy beacon, and thou wilt attain felicity at thine end.

529. Who may be termed most prosperous in his dealings, He who barters the perishable for the everlasting.

530. It is a defect peculiar to this world, that it grants to none his deserts, being either too lavish or too niggard.

531. The machinations of the evil-doer will end in defeat, and expose him to peril.

532. He who makes the service of God his chief pursuit, will enjoy interest without possessing capital.

533. Indifference to this world affords mental ease and corporeal repose, but the allurements of this world produce uneasiness of mind and physical disquietude, and a thorough conviction of God's providence knows no dread of privation, anxiety for sustenance, nor fear of man.

534. He who devotes himself to godliness will escape the cares of this world, and the anxieties regarding the future state.

535. The lot of human nature is perturbation, which crushes the bones and consumes the strength.

536. On being asked to state his circumstances, the sage replied, what can be the condition of him whose existence is perishable, whose health is impaired, and who is vulnerable in his imagined security.

537. Being told of one who had acquired abundant wealth, the sage inquired whether he had also acquired days in which to spend it.

538. It is related, that an Indian king gave one of his pages a mandate, with the injunction to present it to him whenever he observed him under the influence of rage. Its contents were, Cease, for thou art not a god, but a body perishable and self-destructive, soon to return to worms and dust.

539. The king of **Sheba** had a dwarf slave whose presence was desired whenever malefactors were scourged, on those occasions, the dwarf was wont to exclaim, My Lord, remember the day of judgment.

540. A wise man sold his estates for eighty thousand gold deniers. Having been asked, why doest thou not devote the produce to thy children, he replied, I treasure up my wealth with my Creator, and appoint God the treasury for my children, - he had devoted the whole sum to charity.

541. The sage having been told of one who had died in the full vigour of health, replied, can he be deemed healthy about whose neck death is pending.

542. The sage having observed a man dismayed, addressed him to the following effect. If thine anxiety be of this world only, the Creator has anticipated thy relief, and if thy solicitude be of the world to come, may the Creator increase it.

543. When the world is tested by the man of intellect, it will be found an enemy in the guise of friendship.

544. A sage, having been overtaken by sickness, was asked to disclose his affairs, to which he replied, what can be expected from one who sets out on a distant journey without provision, who is about to descend unattended into a pit in the wilderness, or one who is cited to appear before the king and has no defence - assailed by so many calamities, what can be his condition.

545. The querist, however, replied, but how can man remedy these evils, to which the sage rejoined, by attaining much for little, by a consciousness of earthly sorrows, by resisting the allurements of the lesser for the sake of the greater world - he will thus obtain twofold happiness.

546. There was once discovered, in a province of the Roman empire, a stone on which the following inscription was engraved in Roman characters - Son of man, act whilst thou canst, and place thy reliance on God. Let not thine unbridled passion induce thee to sin, neither anticipate care, for if it be destined in thy day, the Creator will bring it despite thy struggles.

547. It proceeded, let not the accumulation of wealth perplex thee, for it is hoarded by many for the future husbands of their wives, and that which man denies to himself often increases the treasures of others. The man of intellect will derive information from these maxims and profit by them.

548. The sage relates, that there was discovered, on the gate of a ruined city in Greece, a stone bearing the following inscription in Greek characters - Son of man, were thy thoughts but directed to the fewness of days yet left to thee, thou wouldst despise the futility of thy desires, moderate thine activity, and circumscribe thy designs, lest remorse overtake thee when thy feet shall totter, when thine household and thine attendants will forsake thee, when thy relatives will abandon thee, when thy friends will neglect thee, and when thou shalt return no more to thine house, and thine avocations shall be beyond thy powers.

549. There was further engraved thereon - Son of man, thou pursuest the transient desires and fleeting pleasures of this world, and seekest to exact its wealth, and thus thou heapest sin on thyself and wealth on thine household, - the former thou carriest to the grave, and the latter thou bequeath Est to thy survivors.

550. A man said to the sage, Alas, how extreme is thy poverty! to which he meekly replied, Couldst thou but define poverty, thou wouldst be concerned more for thine own than for mine.

551. It is related of a sage, who dwelt in a province whose inhabitants were in great distress, but who remained indifferent to the public sorrow, that being asked whether he sympathized with the sufferings of his fellow creatures, no, was his reply. Being interrogated as to the reason, he rejoined, Had this scene appeared to me in a dream, couldst thou imagine that the illusion would have remained on mine awaking, Hence my indifference, for reflection leads me to regard every event in life as a dream, and him alone vigilant who forms a correct notion of human nature, for as the spark is the eye of light, so is the intellect the eye of the soul, and as the sun is the luminary of the universe, so is the soul the light of the body.

552. The following three inscriptions engraved on three tombs, were once discovered in the land of **YASHAE**. The first convoyed the following reflection - Must not the enjoyment of man's life be damped by the consciousness that the Creator will judge his good and evil deeds, and reward him accordingly, The second run thus - How can he taste the sweets of life, who feels that death may suddenly overtake him, remove him from power and dignity, and consign him to that dark abode which has been prepared for him, And the third was - How can he delight in life, whose lot is the dark subterraneous cave, which will pale his features, change his brightness, and consume his flesh and bones.

553. The sage observed, how many enter on a day which they do not see completed, and how many hope for the morrow which, alas! has not been allotted to them.

554. He continued, could man but perceive the casualties of life and its sequel, he would not fail to despise both its wealth and vicissitudes.

555. Alas, said the sage, that man should weary to benefit his heir, or be anxious for that which is the inheritance of the grave.

556. Man, thy happiest position in this world is not without alloy, thou canst not enjoy honey unmixed with venom.

557. When success crowns thine efforts, and rumour declares thy wishes wholly successful, beware of impending reverses.

558. The fear of God is strength and honour, but the result of vain glory is privation and scorn.

Chapter 45

559. Whose cares are the most protracted, the sage replied, His whose daily requirements are his constant anxiety.

560. He who prefers sordidness to the dignity of contentment, or craves for more than he needs, or covets that with which God has favoured others, will meet with endless care and weariness that knows no repose.

561. A sage chanced to pass a certain man, and addressed him thus - How do thy worldly affairs progress, I diligently attend to them. But, continued the sage, has success crowned thine endeavour, no, said the other, but scantily. Well, continued the sage, if thou hast but scantily succeeded in that which thou pursuest so ardently, what canst thou expect in the future state, which thou so utterly neglect.

Chapter 46

562. The sage observes - None is so poor, as he who is discontented with his lot.

563. None is more indigent than he who dreads poverty.

564. Better the grave than a fall to poverty.

565. The sage having been asked how he fared in life, he replied, how can one fare, who has lost his wealth but retained his luxurious habits, **566.** Liberality to another renders thee his superior, independence his equal, respect shown will be reciprocated, and favours solicited will cause thee to be slighted.

567. With the decrease of our wealth our opinions lose their weight, even with our children, who disobey our words and orders.

Chapter 47

568. The sage observes, that favour is valueless which entails humiliation, and calls up the blush of dependence, for the loss must ever exceed the advantage.

569. Of all the bitterness that I have tasted, said the sage, none exceeds that of soliciting favours.

570. The sage was asked what he deemed incurable. He defined it, the favour solicited by the philanthropist, and denied by the sordid.

571. Better submit to privations than solicit a favour of the unworthy, whose refusal but aggravates the humiliation.

572. A man thus addressed the sage - Pray to thy God, that I may not need mankind. No, replied the sage, mutual dependence is indispensable, but I will pray, that thou mayest not need the worthless amongst men.

573. A sage is said to have implored God not to subject him to dependence on mortals, but, continued he, should it be my lot to need thy creatures, grant that it may be the kind-hearted and liberal-minded, whose words are affable

Mivchar HaPeninim

and sweet, and who will not vaunt in my presence of the services they have rendered.

574. The sage impressed on his son, to implore God not to render wicked men indispensable to his existence, for that is the presage of disaster.

575. He who craves for more than he needs or merits deserves a refusal.

576. Avarice engenders disrespect, rashness error, and over-circumspection loss.

577. To solicit from him who procrastinates, and ultimately disappoints, is like seeking favours from a lifeless image.

578. He who asks a favour of the niggard will reap disappointment and incur hatred.

579. He who seeks a favour of the niggard renders himself worse by far than he.

580. The guest of the miser needs not fear nausea, nor will he require medicine.

581. The hospitality of the sordid starves the animal, and the stable will require no cleaning.

582. Tell to me, said a king to his minister, what you consider the greatest of calamities, Poverty, your liege. No, rejoined the king, I

Mivchar HaPeninim

conceive it to be that sordidness which does not quit its followers until they incur disgrace.

583. He who seeks a favour of the avaricious, is like him who attempts to catch fish in the wilderness.

584. The following words were addressed by a philanthropist to his friends - Should you ever need my favour, apply by petition, and not personally, lest your countenance betray the humiliation of soliciting.

585. There is no equivalent for the degradation of seeking favours, though riches may be obtained thereby.

586. Should the humiliation of seeking favours be balanced with the acquired gift, the former is sure to outweigh the latter.

587. Let the applicant for favours address himself to the liberal, kind-hearted, and disinterested, but avoid the mean-spirited, for he will not be gracious at thy request.

Mivchar HaPeninim

Chapter 48

588. Envy is a blemish of the mind.

589. Envy is to the mind, what that disease is to the body which engenders consumption.

590. The sage thus addressed his son - Beware of envy, for thy countenance will betray it, but not that of thine enemy.

591. He continued, Envy inflicts the greatest misery on its votaries, their sadness is perpetual, their soul is grieved, their intellect is dimmed, and their heart disquieted.

592. Every man may enjoy life to his heart's content, save the envious, who delights only in the misfortunes of others.

593. The envious is sinful, for he hates that which God wills, and rebelliously grieves at that which the Creator bestows on others and denies to him.

594. Every animosity may be healed, save that whose source is envy.

595. The days of the envious man are few, for he grieves at that which injures and benefits not, and ultimately perishes by grief.

Mivchar HaPeninim

596. A man addressed his friend in these terms - I do indeed esteem thee. And why not, replied the other, since thou art not my rival, nor my relative or neighbour, and seeing that my livelihood depends on others.

597. Envy not the possession of thy fellow-man, for thou wilt thus render his existence delightful, whilst thine will pass in sadness, grief, and restlessness.

598. We are amply avenged on the envious man, when we see him dejected at our joy and happiness.

Chapter 49

599. The sages observes, He who affects a dignity which he does not possess will be exposed by the test of discrimination.

600. He who plumes himself on that which he possesses not, imagines himself to have vanquished nature, whilst nature in fact has vanquished him, like him who colours his grey hair, but which the least growth will soon expose.

601. It is reproach enough to man, to learn from others those defects which he fails to discern in himself, and to censure others for that from which he cannot claim exemption, and to injure his neighbour.

Chapter 50

602. The sage observes - Intercourse with the wicked injures reputation and leads to a bad end.

603. An evil companion is like a sore disease which ramifies throughout the whole frame, such a companion seeks after the defects of his associate, but conceals his merits.

Chapter 51

604. The sage related, A man having calumniated another in the hearing of an important personage, was thus addressed by him - Thou hast brought to light thine own great defects, by expatiating on the faults of others, for he who goes in quest of the foibles of others, is guided in his search by failings peculiar to himself.

605. A man said to his friend, I will discard thee, for I hear persons speak unfavourably of thee. To which he answered, Didst thou ever hear me asperse them, no, rejoined the other. If so, continued the slandered person, discard the slanderers.

606. A man rebuked his friend in consequence of some evil rumour. The other sought to exonerate himself. But, said the former, my authority is trustworthy. Well, observed the latter, if he were so, he never could have proved a traducer.

607. A man thus addressed his colleague - I have been informed that thou hast censured me. Well, replied the other, this amply proves that thou art a man of greater importance than myself.

Mivchar HaPeninim

608. A man thus addressed his colleague; I learn that thou hast slandered me. No, replied the other, I value myself too much for that.

609. He who lends credence to the slanderer will forfeit the friendship of all, even to the nearest and dearest kinsman.

610. Let no friendship be severed by reason of the calumniator.

611. Expose not the hidden faults of thy fellow-men, lest the Creator bring to light thine, eulogize them when thou mayest, and load them not with the faults peculiar to thyself.

612. He used to say, the bearer of calumny is usually its author.

Chapter 52

613. The sage said, deliver me, O God, from that neighbour whose evil eye watches me and maliciously meditates my injury, who will suppress my merits and expose my failings.

614. The sage was asked to point out the sorest affliction. An evil neighbour, was his reply, for, said he, in thy presence he will harass thee, in thine absence he will malevolently slander and asperse thee.

615. He who patiently endures the injury inflicted by his neighbour will, by the help of God, become the successor of his house.

Chapter 53

616. The sage observes, He who sows discord will reap regret.

617. The sage was asked, how is man to take vengeance on his enemy, by increasing his own good qualities.

618. Beware of enmity, however insignificant, for the smallest insect has often caused the death of the greatest man.

619. There is nothing more dangerous than the hatred of the vile.

Mivchar HaPeninim

Chapter 54

620. The sage observes, five defects are peculiar to the simple only.
    1st. Unreasonable anger.
    2nd. Benevolence ill bestowed.
    3rd. Fruitless exertion.
    4th. Inability to distinguish friend from foe.
    5th. Betrayal of secrets. To those may be added over-haste in replying and over-inquisitiveness.

621. Discretion is the friend of man, folly his adversary.

Chapter 55

622. The sage was wont to observe, the diffident will be encouraged, the proud humbled.

623. He continued, He who relies on his own counsel will err, and he who trusts in his own discretion will stumble.

624. Alas, exclaimed the sage, that man, who must pass through the most loathsome passages, should ever be proud.

625. The arrogant, in his conceit and self-gratulation, over-rates his own merits, - this constitutes pride.

626. The sage was asked to define pride, it is, said he, a folly which its devotees cannot cast off.

Chapter 56

627. In the estimation of the simple, both friend and foe are on a level.

628. Hopeless is that folly which regards mankind without distinction.

629. Who deserves to be held up to scorn. He who assumes a position above his station, he who aspires to a higher place than that assigned to him, and he who dilates on subjects not referred to him.

Mivchar HaPeninim

Chapter 57

630. Regard the fickle-minded rather as an enemy than a friend, and rely not on his friendship.

Chapter 58

631. The sage said, it is wise to discard that friend, who fails to reciprocate thine attention.

Chapter 59

632. The sage saith, He who intrudes on the privacy of others will court contempt by his presence.

633. Dismiss the intruder by withholding from him thine attention.

634. The company of a friend seasons the meal, but the presence of an enemy renders it nauseous.

635. Mankind are disgusted with an idle prattler.

636. A certain king had engraved upon his signet, - Thou becomest tiresome, begone. which ring he exhibited to all intrusive visitors.

637. The sage enjoined his son, to avoid the companionship of the troublesome, for, said he, I have read in medical works, that the society of the intruder, is as intolerable as the tertian ague.

638. When the idle querist intrudes his questions on thee, assume deafness and blindness.

Mivchar　　　　　　　HaPeninim

639. He continued, He ceases to be an intruder, who is conscious of his being tedious.

640. Associate not with the irksome, for such companionship produces vexation.

Chapter 60

641. The sage remarked, He who treats thee pertinaciously will ultimately discard and hate thee.

642. Be not stubborn with the passionate, lest thou entail his guilt also on thyself, nor associate with those who dispute but to oppose.

Chapter 61

643. An ignominious victory is a defeat. Or, the attempt to vanquish the vile enslaves.

644. The sage asked his son, Didst thou ever attempt to vanquish the wicked, yes, said he. To which the father replied, attempt it not, for thou wilt succeed only by becoming viler than he.

Mivchar HaPeninim

Chapter 62

645. Eight persons, said the sage, who, if they incur contempt have to reproach none but themselves.

>**1st**. He who attends a festival uninvited.
>**2nd**. He who assumes command in a house in the presence of its master.
>**3rd**. He who seeks respect from an enemy.
>**4th**. He who solicits a favour from the sordid.
>**5th**. He who pries into the affairs of others.
>**6th**. He who slights the king.
>**7th**. He who aspires to unmerited rank.
>**8th**. And he who addresses a reluctant listener.

Mivchar HaPeninim

Chapter 63

646. The sage observes, Levity banishes respect. Or, banishes the fear of God.

647. The scoffer will be slighted, and the idle prattler will betray himself.

Chapter 64

648. The fleet rider, observed the sage, is not secure from stumbling.

649. Deliberation with the chance of success is preferable to over-haste with the probability of failure.

650. Veracity is the fruit of piety, incessant labour of excessive covetousness, mature deliberation is a tower of strength, and precipitancy a source of regret.

651. An eminent man having been asked, how he attained his honourable position, though of Ethiopian descent, replied, By the utterance of truth, by a strict adherence to fidelity, by abstaining from oppression, and by evincing an indifference to superfluities.

652. The sage concluded, Silence is the most becoming demeanour, discretion the height of humility, whilst prolixity causes unenviable notoriety.

www.ingramcontent.com/pod-product-compliance
Lightning Source LLC
Chambersburg PA
CBHW070146080526
44586CB00015B/1859